NEVER MIND
SUCCESS...
GO FOR
GREATNESS!

Also by Tavis Smiley

On Air*

Empowerment Cards*

Hard Left

How to Make Black America Better

Doing What's Right

Keeping the Faith

*Available from Hay House

Please visit Hay House USA: **www.hayhouse.com**®
Hay House Australia: **www.hayhouse.com.au**
Hay House UK: **www.hayhouse.co.uk**
Hay House South Africa: **orders@psdprom.co.za**

NEVER MIND
SUCCESS...
GO FOR
GREATNESS!

THE BEST ADVICE I'VE EVER RECEIVED

Tavis Smiley

SMILEY BOOKS

Smiley Books,
an imprint of
Hay House, Inc.

Carlsbad, California
Sydney • London • Johannesburg
Vancouver • Hong Kong • New Delhi

Copyright © 2006 by Tavis Smiley

Published in the United States by: Smiley Books, an imprint of Hay House, Inc.

Published and distributed in the United States by: Hay House, Inc.: www.hayhouse.com • **Published and distributed in Australia by:** Hay House Australia Pty. Ltd.: www.hayhouse.com.au • **Published and distributed in the United Kingdom by:** Hay House UK, Ltd.: www.hayhouse.co.uk • **Published and distributed in the Republic of South Africa by:** Hay House SA (Pty), Ltd.: orders@psdprom.co.za • **Distributed in Canada by:** Raincoast: www.raincoast.com • **Published in India by:** Hay House Publishers India: www.hayhouseindia.co.in

Editorial supervision: Jill Kramer • *Design:* Charles McStravick
Photography by: The Smiley Group, Inc./David L. Perry

(Where known, attribution has been given for authors' quotes. In other quotes, italics have been added for emphasis in some instances.)

Library of Congress Control No.: 2005905575

ISBN 13: 978-1-4019-1062-4
ISBN 10: 1-4019-1062-9

10 09 08 07   7 6 5 4
1st printing, January 2006
4th printing, January 2007

Printed in the United States of America

Introduction

As children, we're mindful of grown folks' advice to "eat your vegetables, wash behind your ears, and look both ways." Those simple phrases make us healthy, keep us safe, and last a lifetime. Words inspire us. They challenge us to do better, encourage us when we're sorrowful, and give us hope when there is none.

Many of the quotes that you'll read in this book are those I've collected along the way—some from my readings, some from conversations I've been a part of, and others that I've overheard . . . some from speeches I've listened to, some from those I've given, and some from advice given directly to me. But all scribbled in a little brown book that stays in my bag and goes everywhere I go—the world over.

In this book, you'll also discover some of the best advice ever received by any number of celebrities, artists, authors, politicians, scientists, athletes, thought-leaders, and opinion-makers who've appeared on my PBS TV talk show. After each live taping, I ask my guests for the best advice they've ever received. The answers vary—sometimes funny, sometimes serious, sometimes irreverent, but always interesting and intriguing. I think you'll agree.

It's my hope in the coming years to keep sharing these reflections on life with you in future books, but I hope you'll treasure this first collection just half as much as I do.

All the best . . . and keep the faith!

— **Tavis Smiley,** LOS ANGELES, CALIFORNIA

P.S. I really have to thank my television producer Stephanie Storey for helping me compile all this wonderful advice!

Why be ordinary when you can be extraordinary?

— **India.Arie,** SINGER-SONGWRITER

**A celebrity is someone you want to meet.
A hero is someone you want to be.**

What lies behind us and what lies
before us are tiny matters compared
to what lies within us.

— *Ralph Waldo Emerson*

Remember, we are the ones we've been waiting for.

— **Jim Wallis,** AUTHOR AND MINISTER

We all have a purpose to fulfill.

The will of God will not take you
where the grace of God
cannot keep you.

This too will pass.

— Akiva Goldsman, SCREENWRITER

The difference between
surviving and dying is believing.

— *Noel Jones,* *minister*

There is nothing in life from which
we cannot recover.

— *Susan Taylor,* *author and editor*

No matter what life throws at you—obstacles, downfalls— it's up to you to bounce back.

— **Rachel Elise Rizal,** STUDENT; MEMBER OF ALL-USA HIGH SCHOOL ACADEMIC TEAM

Embarrassments can become testimonies.

You went through something, but don't let something go through you.

All your lessons and appreciations are gained from struggle and strife.

— **Heavy D,** ACTOR AND RAPPER

Leaders are nourished by misfortune.

You have to go through a little hell
to get to heaven.

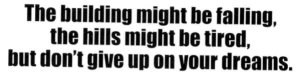

The building might be falling, the hills might be tired, but don't give up on your dreams.

—**Al Green,** MUSICIAN AND MINISTER

The sooner you fall in love with struggle,
the more successful you will be.

It's the *will* of the man,
not the *skill* of the man.

If you keep knocking on doors, someone will eventually open one.

— **Ludacris,** RAPPER AND ACTOR

Sometimes you have to stand on a mountain of *no*'s to get to that one *yes*.

Thou shalt not give up.

Persevere in pursuit of your goals. Ride those highs and lows, but keep at it because you will eventually get there.

— **Shola Lynch**, DOCUMENTARY FILMMAKER

Life is like a heart monitor.
Ups and downs are okay, just don't flatline.

— *Tavis Smiley*

You can have failures and keep going.

If you hang in the barbershop long enough, you're gonna get a haircut.

— **Omarion**, <small>SINGER</small>

Never let go of expectancy.

Whiners don't become winners.

Be positive.

— **Rosanna Arquette,** ACTOR AND FILMMAKER

Why not . . . "Thank God it's Monday"?

Own everything.
That way when you look in the mirror,
all of your shareholders will love you.

Think pink
instead of red.

— **Doris Roberts,** ACTOR

To laugh often and much, to win the respect of intelligent
people and the affection of children, to earn the appreciation
of honest critics, and endure the betrayal of false friends,
to appreciate beauty, to find the best in others, to leave
the world a bit better, whether by a healthy child,
a garden patch . . . to know even one life has breathed
easier because you have lived. This is to have succeeded!

— *Ralph Waldo Emerson*

In life, people can be better or worse for having met you. They may as well be better.

— **Anthony LaPaglia,** ACTOR

One of the greatest myths of our time is that one man can't change the world. In fact, each of us changes the world, which leaves just two questions: *For better or worse? And to what degree?*

What you believe must be borne out by how you behave.

Stay true to your heart,
and do what you know is right.

— **Diahann Carroll**, ACTOR

**It's not about living perfectly,
but living imperfectly with integrity.**

It's not right of might,
but might of right.

— *Gandhi*

Don't act like a man.
Be a man.

— **Sugar Ray Leonard**, BOXER

It's not a question of *what* we want to be when we grow up,
but rather *who* we want to be when we grow up.

It's not just about achieving success, but deserving it.

Too many people are chasing success
but are really looking for significance.

We already have one Stevie Wonder; who are *you* going to be?

— **Brian McKnight,** SINGER-SONGWRITER

Almost everything has been said,
but not by everybody.
Take your turn.

You were born an original;
don't die a cheap copy of somebody else.

Be yourself.
Don't ever try to be
somebody else.

— **Jack Welch**, AUTHOR AND BUSINESS EXECUTIVE

Know who you are.
People crave authenticity.

Write your own obituary,
and then *do* what you want it to say.

Don't spend your life working at a job that you'd rather be retired from.

— **Roger Ebert,** FILM CRITIC

To have it all, you have to
be prepared to have nothing.

— *Noel Jones, minister*

Live like you were dying.

Do everything.
Go out, have a good time,
just don't be stupid.

— **Michael Chiklis,** ACTOR

**There isn't anywhere you have to be tomorrow
that's worth dying for today.**

**Life is short.
Why watch other people doing stuff?**

Be responsible.

Winterize your car.

— Maureen Dowd, COLUMNIST AND AUTHOR

A crust of bread and a corner to sleep in,
A minute to smile and an hour to weep in,
A pint of joy to a peck of trouble,
And never a laugh but the moans come double;
And that's life!

— *Paul Laurence Dunbar, poet*

You should never, ever check out of a motel or hotel without tipping the house-keeper. You may never have laid eyes on them, but they're working very hard.

— **David McCullough,** AUTHOR AND HISTORIAN

The hunter's view of history
is only relevant until the lion has told
its side of the story.

In every person you meet, there's a little piece of God in them, and that's the part you talk to.

— **Terrence Howard,** ACTOR

Never look down on those
who look up to you.

— *Muhammad Ali*

You have two eyes so you can see more. And you have two ears so you can hear more. You have one mouth so you can speak less.

— **Laurence Fishburne**, ACTOR

The less said, the best said.

There's a fine line between off-the-cuff remarks and off-the-wall remarks.

Listen to others with your heart, with passion. It's a lot more meaningful and important than talking.

— **Shohreh Aghdashloo,** ACTOR

What comes from the heart, reaches the heart.

Neither a lofty degree of intelligence,
nor imagination, nor both together
go to the making of genius.
Love, love, love, that is the soul of genius.

— *Wolfgang Amadeus Mozart*

Love somebody.
It never fails.

— **Patricia Raybon,** AUTHOR

To risk loving, knowing that loss is inevitable,
is perhaps the single most important
challenge of our lives.

There is value in belonging
to someone else.

Emphasize the relationship to the human being that you deal with— not his color, not his social status, not his nationality, not his beliefs.

— **Eric Braeden,** ACTOR

It's one thing to hate injustice,
but it's another to love people.

— *Cornel West, author and professor*

Commit to conversation beyond ideology.

Never ask a girl her nationality or her religion before you kiss her.

— **Omar Sharif**, ACTOR

Sometimes it's better
to ask for forgiveness
than permission.

You don't have to say everything you know.

— **Scott Sandage,** AUTHOR AND PROFESSOR

Be a compulsive truth teller.

Don't just say something;
have something to say.

If you see something you don't like, then don't just complain about it. *Do* something about it.

— **Karen Narasaki,** ATTORNEY AND ADVOCATE

**It's better to live for a cause
than to live just because.**

It's not only what we do,
but also what we do not do
for which we are accountable.

— *Molière*

If you don't stand for something, you'll fall for anything.

— **Terry McMillan,** AUTHOR

If you're old enough to be oppressed,
you're old enough to fight oppression.

— *Bernard LaFayette, civil-rights icon*

Are you a victim or a volunteer?

— *Grace Jones, actor and singer*

Jiminy Cricket said, "Always let your conscience be your guide."

— **Tim Robbins,** ACTOR

Some of us must bear the burden
of trying to save the soul of America.

— *Martin Luther King, Jr.*

We all have convictions, but do we have courage?

Stand up and be counted, even if you have to stand alone at first.

— **Theo Milonopoulos,** STUDENT; MEMBER OF ALL-USA HIGH SCHOOL ACADEMIC TEAM

Courage is contagious.

— *Tavis Smiley*

When you break through the brush first, you get the thorns.

To thine own self be true.
Do what you want to do, your way,
on your terms, and be the
authentic person you really are.

— **Halle Berry,** ACTOR

If you think for yourself,
you often think alone.

It takes courage
to cut against the grain.

Stick to your guns.

— **Raul Midon,** MUSICIAN

Provoke and persuade.

Johnny Cash said, "Always tell 'em . . .
if it's all the same to them,
you'd like to try it your way."

— **Billy Bob Thornton**, ACTOR

Be a rebellious individualist.

When people can't see your vision,
sometimes you have to walk.

Always get good shoes.

— Phil Vassar, SINGER-SONGWRITER

If you're leading
and nobody is following,
you're just out for a walk.

You can take your destiny in your own hands. Don't let anybody ever tell you, you can't do what you set out to do.

— **John Singleton,** DIRECTOR AND PRODUCER

When you believe in yourself,
you stay on yourself.

It's always about the future,
not the past.

Always remember the role of history. It's only through that kind of backwards lens that we understand what's happening today.

— **Azadeh Moaveni,** AUTHOR AND JOURNALIST

History is not an accident.
History is a choice.

— *Ossie Davis,* actor and activist

There's a lot of future in your past.

You got what it takes; now go make it happen.

— **BeBe Winans,** SINGER-SONGWRITER

You can jump or get pushed,
but sometimes you just gotta go.

Folk want to *be* something,
but don't want to *do* nothing.

The 7 P's:
Proper prior preparation
prevents piss poor performance.

— **Regina King,** ACTOR

A man asleep can't catch
nothing but a dream.

Hard work spotlights the character of people:
some turn up their sleeves, some turn up their
noses, and some don't turn up at all.

— *Sam Ewig, author*

Can't never did nothing.

— **Nikka Costa,** SINGER-SONGWRITER

Doubt means don't.

Quit quitting.

Know the difference between saying you can't do something and realizing that maybe it's just something you haven't done yet.

— **Michael McDonald,** SINGER-SONGWRITER

The more you can do,
the more you can do.

Don't just sit on the corner;
change the corner where you sit.

On your worst day, help somebody else.

— **Marty Krofft,** TELEVISION PRODUCER

**Change your behavior,
not just your attitude.**

**Don't be so heavenly minded
that you are of no earthly good.**

Did you pray today?

— **Tina Campbell,** SINGER

**Always ask,
"What's the blessing
and what's the lesson?"**

Keep God first.

— **Omar Epps,** ACTOR

See what others don't.
Believe what others won't.

Hope plus faith equals victory.

Anything you want to do, you can do it, as long as you're educated in it.

— S. Epatha Merkerson, ACTOR

I can do anything,
but I cannot do everything.

You can't lead where you don't go.
And you can't teach what you don't know.

Get a great education.

— **Harry Jackson,** MINISTER

Educate a man in mind and not in morals,
and you educate a menace to society.

Some children are trained to be governed;
other children are trained to be governors.

What you earn depends on what you learn.

For career, don't take it personally; treat it like a business. Don't read reviews. Don't worry. Raise the awning at the end of the day and go have dinner.

— **Martin Short,** ACTOR

Measure success by how many people you help make successful.

Aim for the best opportunity, not the best salary.

— *Suze Orman,* author and financial advisor

Watch the money.

— **Daryl Hall,** SINGER-SONGWRITER

I'm not obsessed with money,
but I do rank it right up there
with oxygen.

The three-dollar method:
Every three dollars you get,
you save a dollar, invest a dollar, and
spend a dollar on anything you want.

— **Nelly,** RAPPER AND ACTOR

You can't buy your way into anything
that's worthwhile.

Fame is fleeting.

— **Don Cheadle**, ACTOR AND PRODUCER

Make greatness your claim to fame.
Not fame your claim to greatness.

The road to success is littered
with folk on their way back.

You see the same people going up as you do going down.

— **Taryn Manning,** ACTOR

Most of us are either has-beens,
wannabes, or never weres.

Don't hurt yourself on the way
to where you're going.

Do one thing that scares you every day.

— Cicely Tyson, ACTOR

Celebrate every day that something
has tried to kill you and failed.

— *Lucille Clifton, poet*

Make each day your masterpiece.

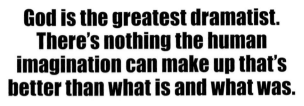

God is the greatest dramatist. There's nothing the human imagination can make up that's better than what is and what was.

— **Ken Burns**,

True artists don't just excite and entertain us, they change how we think and feel.

In the arts, there is always an afterlife.

If you're going to be a writer, make sure that on every page, every character wants something, even if it's only a drink of water.

— **Michael Connelly**, AUTHOR

It's said that when the gazelle wakes up in the morning
he knows there's somebody out there to eat him.
So he'd better wake up running. When the lion wakes up,
he knows if he doesn't catch anything, he'll starve.
So it doesn't matter if you're a gazelle or a lion,
you'd better wake up in the morning running.

Everything comes to he who hustles while he waits.

— **Nick Cannon,** ACTOR

Don't bunt.

Everyone on the planet
was given the same weekend;
some people just use it better.

Life is what you make of it.

— **Matthew Fox,** ACTOR

On our headstone there's a date of birth
and a date of death, but what really counts
is what we do with the dash in the middle.

All will give, but some will give all.

When things are tough and you think things are insurmountable in your life, go out and do something for someone else, and don't ask for anything in return.

— **Jane Seymour**, ACTOR

Sometimes you can make a distinction
without making a difference.
Make a difference.

Some people are long on creed
but short on deed.

Never put yourself above anyone else.

— **Amos Lee**, MUSICIAN

You're either a taker or a caretaker.

Always strive to do better because the people you love deserve the best.

To lead the people, you have to love the people.
And to save the people, you have to serve the people.

— *Cornel West, author and professor*

Make sure you have mercy on people, because you never know when you're going to need a little mercy yourself.

— **Erica Campbell**, SINGER

The toes you step on today may be connected to the behind you have to kiss tomorrow.

— *Quincy Jones, producer and composer*

Be a healer.

Never try to be better than someone else.

— **John Wooden,** BASKETBALL COACH

**Values can actually
enhance value.**

Treat others as you would want to be treated.

— **David Duchovny,** ACTOR AND DIRECTOR

Be generous not greedy,
kind not cruel.

A true friend chastises you in private,
but defends you in public.

Pay attention
to your f---ing wife.
— Ted Danson, ACTOR

Anything you will ever know,
you will learn from someone else.

Our critics are our friends,
for they do show us our faults.

— *Benjamin Franklin*

You don't change people.

— Annette Bening, ACTOR

Love folk anyway.

When you help people feel good about themselves, they'll love you forever.

— Dr. Neil Clark Warren, MATCHMAKER

You only know what you give,
not what they get.

If there be any truer measure of a man
or woman than by what he or she does,
it must be by what he or she gives.

Be funny.

— **Eric Idle,** COMIC

God gave us few geniuses,
but a liberal helping of fools.

Don't let your favorite right be
the right to remain silent.

Boogers and zippers. Check them both before you go onstage.

— **Adam Duritz,** MUSICIAN

Stop striving to impress others, and learn to express yourself.

Sometimes we have to do the things we hate to achieve the things we love.

You're damned if you do, and damned if you don't.

— Sophie Okonedo, ACTOR

The test of a first-rate intelligence is the ability to hold two opposed ideas in mind at the same time and still be able to function.

— *F. Scott Fitzgerald*

Observe.
And from your own observations,
draw your own conclusions.

— **Erika Christensen,** ACTOR

Reexamine your assumptions.

Inspect what you expect.

My grandmother always told me that your assets and your liabilities are the same, depending upon who's judging.

— **Farrah Gray**, AUTHOR AND ENTREPRENEUR

Value is what others think of you,
not what you think of yourself.

People feed pigeons,
but they shoot at eagles.

Nobody can be a better me than I can be.

— Cedric the Entertainer, ACTOR

Create for yourself a place of distinction in this world.

Anyone who amounts to anything is an original.

Never take
anybody's advice.

— **Danny Elfman,** COMPOSER

**Always express
your individuality
with integrity.**

Trust yourself and know yourself.

— **Tracee Ellis Ross**, ACTOR

Do what's right,
even when nobody's looking.

The best ideas can be found in the graveyard,
because too many of us go to our graves
with great ideas that we never act upon.

Believe
in your dreams.

— Marc Forster, DIRECTOR

If nobody has called you high-minded after
sharing your vision, then your vision
ain't big enough.

— Noel Jones, minister

**What are you doing
to deserve your place on earth?**

Go deep inside yourself, find out what really matters and what is true for you, and let that be your path.

— **John Oates,** SINGER-SONGWRITER

People might not listen when you talk, but they can't help it when you sing. So get the world to sing your song.

— *Harry Belafonte, actor and activist*

Don't be incidental or accidental.

— *Ossie Davis, actor and activist*

When you don't know what to do in a given situation, do nothing. Don't try and make it better because you'll probably only make it worse.

— **Minnie Driver**, ACTOR AND SINGER

Insanity is doing the same thing
the same way and expecting
a different result.

You can't be right all the time.

If you know what you want, decisions will be easier to make.

— **Kem**, SINGER-SONGWRITER

A problem is a chance
for you to do your best.

— *Duke Ellington*

All things lead to where you are.

Always follow your instinct.
It will never fail you.

— Isaiah Washington, ACTOR

**All meaningful decisions
are made in your gut,
not in your head.**

**You can believe your way
out of anything.**

Don't give up. There's light at the end of the tunnel.

— **Victor Rivas Rivers,** ACTOR AND AUTHOR

It's not the struggle,
but how we struggle that counts.

What God brings us to,
he brings us through.

As a Black person, you have to do better than anyone else just to be considered equal.

— **Vanessa Williams,** ACTOR AND SINGER

When and where I enter,
the whole race enters with me.

— *Anna Julia Cooper, educator and writer*

Failure is not an option.

Don't give up.
Never, ever give up.

— Burt Reynolds, ACTOR

Be sure that the first line in your will reads:
"Check my pulse again."

— *Warren Buffett, entrepreneur*

Success is the reward for endurance.

YCDA.
You Can Do Anything.

— **Michael Clark Duncan**, ACTOR

The question should be,
is it worth trying to do, not can it be done.

— *Allard Lowenstein, activist*

**Sometimes oversized ambition is the only way
to achieve something extraordinary.**

Always put your name above anything that you create, because someday it's going to be worth something.

— **Sid Krofft,** TELEVISION PRODUCER

Success can be
harder than failure.

Don't confuse the applause
with the cause.

Find something you love to do and devote your life to it.

— **Moby**, SINGER-SONGWRITER

Do what you love and
you will triumph.

Live your legacy.

Be authentic and the universe will handle the details.

— **Jill Nelson,** AUTHOR

We are just vessels in whom
much has been vested.

It's not about what you have,
but who you are.

You either have
to have f--- you money,
or a f--- you attitude.

— **Steven Bochco**, TELEVISION PRODUCER

**Sometimes you have to keep one foot
planted firmly on the ground,
and the other up someone's behind.**

Never take *no* from anyone who
doesn't have the power to tell you *yes*.

— *Alpha Blackburn*, designer

Read the contracts.

— Kelvin "Pos" Mercer, MUSICIAN

It's okay to say,
"I don't know."

Rewrite the rules.

Two wrongs don't make a right, but it'll damn sure get your money back.

— **Erykah Badu**, SINGER-SONGWRITER

If you see me in a fight with a bear, you help the bear. In fact, you can pour honey all over me, and you'd still better help the bear.

What matters is whether you win or lose, *and* how you play the game.

Always keep your hands up and your chin down.

— Ronald "Winky" Wright, BOXER

A winner knows what to do when he's losing.

I always read the sports pages first
because they talk of man's accomplishments
rather than his failures.

— *Earl Warren*, *former Chief Justice of the U.S. Supreme Court*

Don't be the last one at the party.

— **Miss Shabazz,** ACTIVIST

There's nothing wrong
with being the first one,
just don't be the last one.

Al Pacino told me, don't ever be naked.
Don't ever do full frontal.
He said you've got to keep
a little mystery to yourself.

— **John Leguizamo**, ACTOR

The press is like a man,
the more you say no,
the more they want you.

Public appearances should be brief and rare.

— *Nat King Cole,* musician

Never get caught acting.

— Amber Tamblyn, ACTOR

Life is a perpetual audition.

If you're going to stand, stand.
If you're going to sit, sit.
But don't wobble.

Say what you mean, mean what you say, and don't be mean.

— **Mos Def**, MUSICIAN AND ACTOR

When you *know* better, you should *do* better.

Some folk are about as slick as sandpaper and about as subtle as pepper spray.

Don't make easy alliances. Very often the first person that approaches you is approaching you because everybody else in the community hates them.

— **John Sayles,** WRITER AND DIRECTOR

You can't be afraid to make some enemies.

All my skinfolk,
ain't my kinfolk.

— *Zora Neale Hurston, author*

Do not give people the benefit of the doubt. Start everyone at zero. Either they gain points with you or they lose points with you. Give people the benefit of the doubt and you usually get hurt.

— **Ice Cube,** ACTOR AND RAPPER

Sometimes you can be so open-minded,
your brains fall out.

Don't let others make assumptions
about your life.

Never confuse what you have with who you are.

— **Janis Kearney,** AUTHOR AND PRESIDENTIAL DIARIST

It's not about it; it's about you.

Stuff.
It's nice to have,
but it's nicer to be free from it.

Nothing's free.

— **Mark Harmon,** ACTOR

Money is not meaning.

Always take
your wallet onstage.

— **Bill Maher,** COMIC AND AUTHOR

Always take
your purse onstage.

— *Aretha Franklin,* singer-songwriter

Always sign your own checks.

— **Chilli**, SINGER

At some point, help becomes a handicap.

At the banquet table of life, there are no reserved seats. You get what you can take and you keep what you can hold. If you can't take anything, you won't get anything. And if you can't hold anything, you won't keep anything. And you can't take anything without organization.

— *A. Philip Randolph, civil-rights leader*

Be professional.

— Garcelle Beauvais-Nilon, ACTOR

You will never be promoted until you become
overqualified for the job you already have.

Sometimes it's not about how well you do your job.
It's about how long you can survive
the politics of your work environment.

If people are talking well of you, that's good. If they speak bad of you, that's not necessarily bad. It's when they stop speaking that you have to worry.

— **Craig Brewer,** FILMMAKER

I'd rather be looked
over than overlooked.

Never mind the chattering class.

You don't have to blow out my candle to make yours burn brighter.

— Bob Eubanks, TELEVISION HOST

Peacocks strut
because they can't fly.

Great spirits often encounter
violent opposition from mediocre minds.

— Albert Einstein

When someone is trying to intimidate you, it seems like they're coming from a place of power, but really they're coming from a place of weakness. So, remember that and don't let them make you feel small.

— **Cynthia Nixon,** ACTOR

The heart that's afraid of trying never learns to dance
The dream that's afraid of waking never takes a chance
The one who's afraid of being taken never learns to give
The soul afraid of dying never learns to live.

— *Amanda McBroom, songwriter*

If anybody ever says that won't work, run from them.

— **Robert Hudson**, DOCUMENTARY FILMMAKER (left)

**Rebel against anyone
who says you can't.**

Failing does not make you a failure.

Respect yourself.

— **T-Boz**, SINGER

The high trees get the wind.

Your detractors have a right to be wrong.

Don't let the bastards get you down.

— **Norm Stamper,** POLICE CHIEF AND AUTHOR

It's one thing to let folk get on your last nerve,
just don't let them get on your reserve nerve.

You're either up, or getting up.
You're never down.

Never take a step backwards, not even to gain momentum.

— **Andy Garcia**, ACTOR

**Constant motion
does not necessarily mean
forward motion.**

When you rest, you rust.

The best advice I ever received was from my daughter. I was fiddling with my cell phone, doing about ten things at the same time. She looked at me and said, "Dad, you really should learn how to listen."

— **Alex Gibney**, DOCUMENTARY FILMMAKER

The sun doesn't rise and set around you.
And if you think it does,
you're bound to get sunburned.

A baby's birth is God's way of saying
you have permission to continue.

Treat everybody just like you treat people in your hometown. The rest of the world wants that same smile, that same courtesy, that same compassion.

— **Lionel Richie,** SINGER-SONGWRITER

Sometimes you have to treat people differently to treat them equally.

This is something that came from my mom when I was little. I remember asking her about men and boys, and she said, "I've got one piece of advice. If they don't open the door for you, they're not worth anything."

— **LeAnn Rimes,** SINGER

When you're taken for granted,
you're taken.

Be firm, but fair.

Nothing will ever taste as good as it feels to be thin.

— **Mike Huckabee**, GOVERNOR OF ARKANSAS

I'm in pretty good shape
for the shape I'm in.

Where are you on your priority list?

Moisturize, moisturize, moisturize.

— Jon Cryer, ACTOR

Don't just mop up the water; turn off the faucet.

Always do things in addition to, not instead of.

Find out whatever it is you're really, really good at and do it anyway, whether you make a living at it or not.

— **Drew Carey,** COMIC

Compete only with yourself and your own legacy.

Be the best version of yourself you can possibly be.

— **Margaret Wertheim,** <small>COLUMNIST</small>

There will never be another one just like you.

Even when you are gifted, you still have to grow.

Whenever you want to blame someone, remember it's not about them. It's about you.

— **Alanis Morissette,** SINGER-SONGWRITER

It's all about how you look at it.
The world continues to rotate
even when you're standing still.

Try to take the beam out of your own eye before you go looking for splinters in somebody else's.

— **Roseanne Barr,** COMEDIAN AND ACTOR

Judgment only looks good in retrospect.

There can be no dichotomy between what we do and what we believe. We must always do what we believe.

— *Benjamin E. Mays, educator*

Figure out what you love to do more than anything in the world, come up with a way to get paid for it, and you will have life right by the throat.

— **Pat Williams,** SPORTS EXECUTIVE

Follow your smile.

Remain inspired, not retired.

E. L. Doctorow said that writing is like driving at night with the headlights on. You can only see a little ways in front of you, but you can make the whole journey that way.

— **Anne Lamott,** AUTHOR

Take life by the yard,
it's hard.
Take it by the inch,
it's a cinch.

Stop drinking.

— **Karl Fleming,** JOURNALIST AND AUTHOR

Don't profane God's creation.

Thank God for a statute of limitations
on stupidity.

Don't take no wooden nickels.

— **John Legend,** SINGER-SONGWRITER

Figures don't lie,
but liars can figure.

One man's verisimilitude
is another man's fakery.

Act better than you feel.

— Carrie Fisher, ACTOR AND AUTHOR

Never ignore an inner voice
that tells you something can be better
even when other people tell you it's okay.

— *Frank Sinatra*

Be a witness.

Winston Churchill said, "When you're going through hell, keep going."

— **Bebe Moore Campbell,** AUTHOR

Get better, don't get over.

— *Quincy Jones, producer and composer*

Life is best lived with a sense of perspective that only the constant awareness of death can bring.

Don't look too far for happiness. The diamond is right in your backyard.

— **George Pelecanos,** AUTHOR

Excellence is the result of caring more than others think is wise, risking more than others think is safe, dreaming more than others think is practical, and expecting more than others think is possible.

Sorrow looks back, worry looks around, but faith looks up.

Don't be so discouraged.
— Joyce Carol Oates, AUTHOR

**Some folk think their job
is to stop you from doing yours.**

Always ask, "Did I give it my best?"

You don't want ten years to pass and say, "What if I would've tried that?" So if you believe something in your heart, have the gumption to go out and try to make it happen. Even if it doesn't work out, you can look at yourself in the mirror and know you gave it a shot.

— **Jimmy Smits**, ACTOR

Sometimes the worst risk is not taking one.

Use what you got,
while you still got it to use.

Accept the self you are with all of your limitations, and then within those limits be all that you can be.

— **John Shelby Spong,** MINISTER AND AUTHOR

Know your strengths and your abilities, your weaknesses and your limitations.

— *Tavis Smiley*

**Don't just *be* something.
Do something.**

Writers are like jazz musicians. If you're going to be a good writer, you have to write. Write every day, until someone is ready to pay you for it.

— **Bakari Kitwana,** AUTHOR

Instead of being motivated by ambition,
be motivated by challenge.

Learn something every day.

— **Steven Levitt,** ECONOMIST AND AUTHOR

The more you know,
the more you owe.

Revel in human endeavor.

If you don't live it,
don't write it.

— **Shelby Lynne**,

Inspiration is everywhere.

Take your time and enjoy life.

— **Malcolm Jamal-Warner,** ACTOR

Die empty.

There's a difference between being driven and being a workaholic.

Don't become addicted to the work.

— **Laura Linney,** ACTOR

It's not about the work you do,
but about the work you get done.

Conquest without contribution
is meaningless.

Don't take yourself so seriously.
— **LeVar Burton**, ACTOR

Always remain
un-self-conscious.

Before honor comes humility.

Apologize early and often.

— **Bobby Houston,** DOCUMENTARY FILMMAKER

Getting it right means acknowledging what went wrong.

Get down where you get mad.

— *Wren T. Brown, actor*

Do not take things personally.

— **Alfre Woodard**, ACTOR

Sometimes the things we need to know
aren't the things we want to hear.

Win like a champion;
lose like a champion.

Rudyard Kipling said to learn to recognize our successes and our failures as the twin imposters that they are.

— **Oliver Platt,** ACTOR

The worth of a life cannot be found in a single failure or a solitary success.

It's not thy Thingdom come,
but thy Kingdom come.
Seek something higher.

— *Ruby Dee,* actor and activist

Dream big.

— Djimon Hounsou, ACTOR

Don't be a profile in timidity.

How will history remember you?

If you will it, it is not a dream.

— **Henry Winkler,** ACTOR AND AUTHOR

We know what we are,
but know not what we may be.

— *William Shakespeare*

**Our lives are not so much made up
of the breaths that we take,
but of the moments that take our breath away.**

About the Author

With his late-night television talk show, *Tavis Smiley,* on PBS, and his radio show *The Tavis Smiley Show from NPR,* Smiley was the first American ever to simultaneously host signature talk shows on both PBS and National Public Radio. Smiley's television program is the first show in the history of PBS to be broadcast from the West Coast. *The Tavis Smiley Show* on public radio is currently distributed by PRI, Public Radio International. He can also be heard weekdays on his nationally syndicated commentary, *The Smiley Report.* Additionally, Tavis offers political commentary on the nationally syndicated *Tom Joyner Morning Show.*

Tavis has authored nine books, including *On Air* and *Keeping the Faith,* an inspiring collection of personal narratives about love, loss, and faith by African Americans from all walks of life. He's also the founder of the Tavis Smiley Foundation.

Website: **www.TavisTalks.com**

We hoped you enjoyed this Smiley Books/Hay House book.
If you'd like to receive additional information, please contact:

Hay House, Inc.
P.O. Box 5100
Carlsbad, CA 92018-5100

(760) 431-7695 or **(800) 654-5126**
(760) 431-6948 (fax) or **(800) 650-5115 (fax)**
www.hayhouse.com® • **www.hayfoundation.org**

Distributed in Australia by:
Hay House Australia Pty. Ltd., 18/36 Ralph St. • Alexandria NSW 2015 •
Phone: 612-966299 • Fax: 69-412-9669-4144 • www.hayhouse.com.au

Distributed in the United Kingdom by:
Hay House UK, Ltd., 292B Kensal Rd., London W10 5BE • Phone:
44-20-8962-1230 • Fax: 44-20-8962-1239 • www.hayhouse.co.uk

Distributed in the Republic of South Africa by:
Hay House SA (Pty), Ltd., P.O. Box 990, Witkoppen 2068 •
Phone/Fax: 27-11-706-6612 • orders@psdprom.co.za

Distributed in India by: Hay House Publishers India,
Muskaan Complex, Plot No. 3, B-2, Vasant Kunj, New Delhi 110 070 •
Phone: 91-11-4176-1620 • Fax: 91-11-4176-1630 • www.hayhouseindia.co.in

Distributed in Canada by: Raincoast, 9050 Shaughnessy St.,
Vancouver, B.C. V6P 6E5 • Phone: (604) 323-7100 •
Fax: (604) 323-2600 • www.raincoast.com

Tune in to **HayHouseRadio.com®** for the best in inspirational talk radio featuring
top Hay House authors! And, sign up via the Hay House USA Website to receive the
Hay House online newsletter and stay informed about what's going on with your
favorite authors. You'll receive bimonthly announcements about: Discounts and
Offers, Special Events, Product Highlights, Free Excerpts, Giveaways, and more!
www.hayhouse.com®